Extreme Bridges

ANN O. SQUIRE

Children's Press®
An Imprint of Scholastic Inc.
New York   Toronto   London   Auckland   Sydney
Mexico City   New Delhi   Hong Kong
Danbury, Connecticut

Content Editor
Robert Wolffe, EdD
Professor
Bradley University, Peoria, Illinois

Library of Congress Cataloging-in-Publication Data
Squire, Ann, author.
 Extreme bridges / by Ann O. Squire.
   pages cm. — (A true book)
 Audience: 9–12.
 Audience: Grade 4 to 6.
 Includes bibliographical references and index.
 ISBN 978-0-531-20745-1 (library binding : alk. paper) — ISBN 978-0-531-21556-2 (pbk. : alk. paper)
 1. Bridges—Juvenile literature. 2. Civil engineering—Juvenile literature. I. Title.
 TG148.S68 2015
 624.2—dc23   2014005454

All rights reserved. Published in 2015 by Children's Press, an imprint of Scholastic Inc.
Printed in China 62
SCHOLASTIC, CHILDREN'S PRESS, A TRUE BOOK™, and associated logos are trademarks and/or registered trademarks of Scholastic Inc.

1 2 3 4 5 6 7 8 9 10 R 24 23 22 21 20 19 18 17 16 15

Front cover: Hoover Dam Bypass under construction

Back cover: Person crossing suspended footbridge over Hunza River in Pakistan

Find the Truth!

Everything you are about to read is true *except* for one of the sentences on this page.

Which one is **TRUE**?

T or F The arch bridge is one of the oldest bridge designs.

T or F The Golden Gate Bridge is the world's longest suspension bridge.

Find the answers in this book.

Contents

THE **BIG** TRUTH!

Basic Bridge Types

Tree roots can be trained to grow into a sturdy bridge.

The Golden Gate Bridge has been closed because of weather three times.

6

CHAPTER 1

Weird and Wonderful Bridges

Bridges help us get from place to place. And some bridges do so in truly extreme ways. Sometimes, it is a bridge's size or shape that makes it extreme. Other times, a person can feel extreme just by being on the bridge. Cross France's Millau Viaduct and you'll be a dizzy 909 feet (277 meters) above the valley below. Mexico's Baluarte Bridge is even higher, at 1,322 feet (403 m) above the ground.

The Millau Viaduct is a cable-stayed bridge, a bridge type related to **suspension** bridges.

7

Magdeburg Water Bridge

It is not unusual for cars, trains, and people to use a bridge. What about a bridge for boats? The Magdeburg Water Bridge is an **aqueduct** in Germany. It crosses over the Elbe River and links two canals. At 3,012 feet (918 m) long, it is the longest water bridge in the world. The bridge is wide and deep enough for huge ships and barges to cross.

The Magdeburg Water Bridge took six years and about $700 million to build.

It takes less than 10 minutes for the Rolling Bridge to unroll.

London's Rolling Bridge

One of the world's most unusual bridges is the **pedestrian** Rolling Bridge in London. For most of the week, the bridge is curled up in an octagon shape next to the Grand Union Canal. Rolled up, it looks more like a modern sculpture than a bridge. Every Friday at noon, bridge workers operate controls that unroll the bridge over the canal. After people cross back and forth, the workers flip a switch, and the bridge rolls up again.

Some root bridges can support the weight of 50 people or more at one time!

Living Bridges

Most bridges are lumber, stone, concrete, or steel. The War-Khasis tribe of northern India uses a more unusual material: tree roots. The rubber trees in this warm, wet region have incredibly strong root systems. With hollow tree trunks as guides, the roots are trained to grow across the river. When they reach the other side, the roots burrow into the ground. After 10 to 15 years, a "living bridge" is formed.

Sundial Bridge

When is a bridge more than a bridge? When it also tells time. The Turtle Bay Sundial Bridge in Redding, California, has a 217-foot-tall (66 m) support tower that points in a true north-south direction. The tower casts its shadow on a large dial to the north of the bridge. As the sun crosses the sky during the day, the tower's shadow moves along the dial. This makes the bridge the largest working sundial in the world.

The Sundial Bridge's tower is tall and angled to cast a long shadow for the sundial.

A Batty Bridge

If you walk or drive across the Congress Avenue Bridge in Austin, Texas, during daylight hours, you won't notice anything special about it. But this bridge has a secret. From mid-March until November, it is home to 1.5 million Mexican free-tailed bats! During the day, the bats roost upside down underneath the bridge's roadway. At dusk every evening, they begin to stir. Night is hunting time for these flying animals.

A cloud of bats emerges from underneath the Congress Avenue Bridge.

People often line the Congress Avenue Bridge to watch the bats come out.

With a whooshing of wings, the entire bat colony emerges from beneath the bridge in search of food. Every night, the bats consume up to 30,000 pounds (13,608 kilograms) of insects. Many of these are agricultural pests, so the Austin bats are a real help to local farmers and the environment. By providing the bats a place to live, the bridge is doing its part as well.

Rope bridges are still in use in many places around the world.

CHAPTER 2

The First Bridges

Unlike freeways, skyscrapers, and railroads, bridges are not a modern invention. Imagine a group of early hunters moving through the forest in search of food. Suddenly, a deep, rushing stream blocks their way. To reach the other side, they might pile stones in the streambed to form a path. Or if they are lucky, they may find a fallen tree that they can drag into position and use as a walkway across the water.

Rope bridges are a type of suspension bridge.

15

An early bridge could easily be a conveniently placed fallen tree.

Early Crossings

Early humans later built rough bridges to cross rivers and streams. They sometimes tied wooden planks together to stretch across larger bodies of water. Vines and other plant materials could be woven together to create bridges for crossing deep ravines. Although today's bridges are marvels of modern engineering, they all have their roots in the early bridges built by our ancestors.

Crafting Today's Bridges

The earliest bridges could only span short distances. To cross wide distances, bridges needed to be stronger and sturdier. They had to support weight, even in the middle of a wide canyon and high above the ground. Engineers have found many ways to solve these issues. Vines and wood were replaced with stronger materials, such as metals. Short pins called rivets hold pieces together. Other bridges are made stronger by their shape, such as arches.

Many modern bridge designers take pride in making their bridges beautiful as well as useful. The Nanzhonghuang Bridge in Taiyuan, China, is one example.

Beam Bridges

When our ancestors laid a tree trunk across a stream, they were constructing one of the most basic types of bridge: the beam bridge. All you need to build this bridge is a **rigid** structure, such as a tree trunk, and two supports at each end to rest it on. To build a longer bridge, a designer adds more supports. Beam bridges may be simple, but they are effective. In fact, beam bridges rank among today's longest bridges.

Beam bridges are generally the least expensive bridges to build.

Crossing Lake Pontchartrain

The longest bridge in the United States is a beam bridge. The Lake Pontchartrain Causeway is a 24-mile-long (39 kilometer) bridge that crosses a huge lake in Louisiana. The bridge is supported by more than 9,000 concrete **pilings**. The causeway is not only the longest bridge in the United States. It is also the longest bridge in the world that runs continuously over water.

The Lake Pontchartrain Causeway is actually two separate bridges side by side. One bridge carries northbound traffic. The other carries cars going south.

The Tianjin Grand Bridge is one of the longest bridges in the world.

World's Longest

Two of the longest bridges in the world are also beam bridges for most of their lengths. The Tianjin Grand Bridge carries high-speed trains in China. At 71 miles (114 km) long, the Tianjin Grand Bridge was the world's longest bridge when it was completed in 2010. It lost that title the next year, when the Danyang-Kunshan Grand Bridge opened in China. This superlong railway bridge stretches for 102 miles (164 km)!

A series of concrete supports holds up the Danyang-Kunshan Grand Bridge for much of its length.

Building the Danyang-Kunshan Grand Bridge was a huge project. It took four years and more than 10,000 workers to complete it. The cost was an amazing $8.5 billion! Both this bridge and the Tianjin Grand Bridge have short portions that use suspension bridge designs. This allows the roadway to be higher in these sections with plenty of room between bridge supports so ships can pass underneath.

Live Load, Dead Load

Bridge designers must consider the weight of the vehicles and other traffic that cross a bridge. This weight makes up a bridge's live load. Designers also worry about dead load, or the weight of the bridge itself. This is generally not a problem in short bridges. But the longer a bridge is, the heavier it is. To minimize dead load, designers have used a variety of materials and shapes to make a bridge lighter while keeping it safe and strong.

Cables provide some support in a cable-stayed bridge, so fewer towers are needed and the bridge is lighter.

23

Basic Bridge Types

Most of the world's bridges can be divided into a few basic types. Each type has its own shape and method for supporting weight. Some bridge types, such as beam bridges and **truss** bridges, are closely related. Others are very different from each other.

BRIDGE TYPE	BASIC APPEARANCE	FIRST USED	HOW IT WORKS
Beam		Ancient times	Roadway rests on two or more support beams
Suspension		Ancient times	Roadway hangs from two main cables; weight is transferred along the main cables to supporting towers
Arch		In use more than 2,000 years	Weight distributed along the curve of a bridge's arch or arches and to the ground
Truss		Early designs date back to the 15th century	Weight distributed along network of braces, or supports
Cable-Stayed		First "true" cable-stayed bridges built mid-20th century	Roadway anchored to one or more towers by series of cables

Trusses help make a stronger, lighter bridge.

Trusses and Arches

Bridge designers have multiple choices when they want to build a long and strong beam bridge. One is to add lots of supports, as the designers of the Lake Pontchartrain Causeway did. Another option is to add a network of braces, called a truss. Sometimes the truss is placed above the roadway, and sometimes it is below. Either way, it serves the same purpose: to strengthen the bridge and allow it to span a greater distance.

Most truss bridges built today are steel.

Heavy Metal

The world's longest truss bridge is the Ikitsuki Bridge in Nagasaki, Japan. It measures 1,312 feet (400 m). This is not nearly as long as other record-setting bridges. Why? Trusses face serious design issues in superlong bridges. For a short bridge, a small and simple truss is enough. But as a bridge gets bigger and longer, it requires a larger truss. Eventually, the truss would have to be too large to affordably build and maintain.

The Ikitsuki Bridge makes it possible to drive from Japan's mainland to the island of Ikitsuki.

The Pont du Gard carried millions of gallons of water to nearby residents every day.

Arch Bridges

Some of history's greatest bridge builders were the ancient Romans. They played a large part in developing the use of arches to support bridges. Arch bridges are very strong. The weight is distributed along the curve of the arch down to sturdy supports, called **abutments,** at each end. Many ancient Roman arch bridges are still standing today. One of the most famous is the Pont du Gard aqueduct in France, constructed in the first century CE.

Some researchers argue rainbow bridges were named for their rainbowlike shape.

Rainbow Bridges

Other ancient bridges are a bit mysterious. First built in China in the 1030s, rainbow bridges were built by weaving together short pieces of wood. Pieces were tied together using bamboo. Once completed, the bridge formed a high arch over a river. Boats could pass underneath it easily. No examples of this wooden arch bridge exist today. The only remaining image is in a painted scroll from the late 11th century.

Researchers can glimpse how rainbow bridges worked by looking at Min-zhe timber arch bridges. They are closely related to rainbow bridges. Both types are built by weaving together pieces of wood. However, Min-zhe bridges are held together by interlocking pieces, not bamboo. Also, on top of each Min-zhe bridge is a covering "house." Many of these bridges are several hundred years old. Locals often use them as meeting places or as the sites of festivals and celebrations.

Today, China's timber arch bridges are still built by hand.

A Major Project

A more modern arch bridge is the Hoover Dam Bypass bridge. This bridge crosses the Black Canyon about 900 feet (274 m) above the Colorado River near Hoover Dam. The desert heat proved a major challenge to construction. It was difficult to pour concrete during the day, so workers poured it at night. During the summer, the concrete was cooled with extra-cold liquid nitrogen. This allowed the concrete to cool at the proper rate to keep it from losing strength.

The Hoover Dam Bypass bridge opened in 2010.

Make an Arch Bridge

The abutments on either end of an arch bridge are very important. To see why, try an experiment. Cut a piece of cardboard or heavy paper into a long, wide strip. Gently bend it into an arch shape and place it on a tabletop. Press down on the arch with your hand. What happens? The arch collapses.

Now add abutments. Place the arch on the table and put a stack of books at each end. Now press on the arch. What happens? The books serve as supports, preventing the arch's ends from spreading apart.

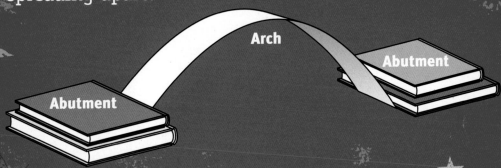

Arch

Abutment

Abutment

The Széchenyi Chain Bridge connects the Pest and Buda sections of Budapest, the capital of Hungary.

CHAPTER 5

Suspension Bridges

Some of the most famous bridges in the world are suspension bridges. These include the Golden Gate Bridge in San Francisco, California, and New York City's Brooklyn Bridge. A beam bridge is supported from below. However, a suspension bridge uses two tall towers and strong cables to suspend, or hang, the roadway from above. At each end of the bridge, the cables are anchored into huge blocks of concrete or stone.

The Széchenyi Chain Bridge was the second permanent crossing built over the Danube River.

Strong and Light

Suspension bridges are among the world's most graceful and elegant bridges. They are very strong and flexible. They can also be much more lightweight than other types of bridges. Some suspension bridges span distances of thousands of feet. It is no wonder they are one of the most common bridge designs.

The Clifton Suspension Bridge was originally designed to carry horse-drawn vehicles.

The Clifton Suspension Bridge in Britain was completed in 1864, after more than 30 years of construction.

The Golden Gate Bridge has become a symbol of San Francisco, California.

The Golden Gate Bridge

It's not the longest, highest, or newest. But the Golden Gate Bridge is one of the world's most recognizable bridges. It is painted bright orange, which helps it blend in with the color of nearby hills. The bridge spans the Golden Gate Strait. This is the entrance to San Francisco Bay from the Pacific Ocean. During construction between 1933 and 1937, a safety net was suspended underneath the bridge. Nineteen workers fell from the bridge and were saved by the net!

The Brooklyn Bridge connects the island of Manhattan to the mainland at Brooklyn, New York.

The Brooklyn Bridge

The Brooklyn Bridge spans New York's East River. Opened in 1883, it was the first suspension bridge to use steel cables to suspend the roadway. Building the bridge took 14 years. To build the foundation, workers had to dig into the muddy river bottom. They descended in airtight capsules and worked inside huge wooden boxes called **caissons**. The caissons were filled with compressed air so the men could breathe.

Elephants on the Bridge

When the Brooklyn Bridge opened, people wondered if such a long bridge was safe. To prove its strength and safety—and to spread word about his circus—showman P. T. Barnum offered to lead a herd of elephants across the bridge. On May 17, 1884, 21 elephants and 17 camels shuffled across the bridge. New Yorkers were convinced. More than 100 years later, the Brooklyn Bridge is still standing.

Crowds of people came to watch P. T. Barnum and his animals cross the Brooklyn Bridge.

When Bridges Fail

Bridge designers must make sure their designs are strong. Bridges do not just need to support any vehicles or people crossing. Depending on a bridge's location, it may also need to stand up to extreme events, such as earthquakes, hurricanes, and severe winds. Most of the time, designers get it right. But sometimes they don't. When problems occur, engineers closely study what went wrong and why, to make sure the issues don't happen again.

Timeline of Extreme Bridges

FIRST CENTURY CE

Pont du Gard is built.

1883

The Brooklyn Bridge opens.

July 1940 marked the opening of the Tacoma Narrows Bridge. This suspension bridge crossed Puget Sound at Tacoma, Washington. People loved the new bridge, but they noticed something strange about it. On windy days, the roadway would "bounce" up and down. Bridge workers complained that the motion made them sick. People nicknamed the bridge Galloping Gertie.

1937
The Golden Gate Bridge opens.

NOVEMBER 1940

The Tacoma Narrows Bridge collapses, six months after its completion.

41

The Tacoma Narrows Bridge was closed to traffic about an hour before it collapsed.

Engineers spent the next four months searching for ways to fix the bridge's bounce. Then in November, a windstorm occurred. Strong winds hit the bridge sideways, and the structure began to gallop and twist. Officials closed the bridge for safety. Then a huge section of the center span broke away with a roar. The remains of the bridge are still at the bottom of Puget Sound. They form one of the largest human-made reefs in the world.

Standing Up to Nature

The Tacoma Narrows Bridge disaster was a difficult learning experience. Today, suspension bridges are designed to better stand up to nature's forces. For example, Japan's Akashi-Kaikyo Bridge spans an amazing 12,828 feet (3,910 m). Despite its length, the bridge is incredibly stable. During construction, a severe earthquake hit the area. The bridge was not seriously damaged, and construction continued. With technology constantly improving, bridges are bound to be even more extreme in the future! ★

The Akashi-Kaikyo Bridge is the world's longest suspension bridge.

43

True Statistics

Number of vehicles to cross the George Washington Bridge each year: 102 million

Number of rivets in the two towers of the Golden Gate Bridge: 1.2 million

Weight of the steel in the Danyang-Kunshan Bridge: 900 million lb. (408 million kg)

Height of West Virginia's New River Gorge Bridge, one of the world's longest arch bridges: 876 ft. (267 m) above the water

Total length of wire used in the Golden Gate Bridge's suspension cables: 80,000 mi. (128,748 km)

Number of people killed in the 1940 Tacoma Narrows Bridge collapse: Zero

Did you find the truth?

T The arch bridge is one of the oldest bridge designs.

F The Golden Gate Bridge is the world's longest suspension bridge.

Resources

Books

Griffiths, Rachel. *Why Do Bridges Arch?* New York: Cambridge University Press, 2010.

Latham, Donna. *Bridges and Tunnels: Investigate Feats of Engineering.* White River Junction, VT: Nomad Press, 2012.

Important Words

abutments (uh-BUHT-muhnts) — the parts of structures that directly receive pressure or weight

aqueduct (AK-wuh-duhkt) — a human-made channel or bridge designed to carry water over valleys and rivers

caissons (KAY-suhnz) — watertight chambers used in construction work underwater or as a foundation

dissolve (di-ZAHLV) — to mix with a liquid and become part of the liquid

pedestrian (puh-DES-tree-uhn) — a person who travels on foot

pilings (PILE-ingz) — heavy wood or steel beams that are driven into the ground to support a bridge or other structure

rigid (RIJ-id) — stiff and difficult to bend or move

suspension (suh-SPEN-shuhn) — a suspension bridge is hung from cables or chains strung from towers

truss (TRUHS) — a strong frame of beams, bars, or rods that supports a roof or bridge

Index

Page numbers in **bold** indicate illustrations

About the Author

Ann O. Squire is a psychologist and an animal behaviorist. Before becoming a writer, she studied the behavior of rats, tropical fish in the Caribbean, and electric fish from central Africa. Her favorite part of being a writer is the chance to learn as much as she can about all sorts of topics. In addition to the Extreme Science books, Dr. Squire has written about many different animals, from lemmings to leopards and cicadas to cheetahs. She lives in Long Island City, New York.

[9]